I0478566

MONEY MAKES THE WORLD GO 'ROUND

BY THE SAME AUTHOR

At Sea
True Loves
Love Finds a Way
It Could Be Worse

MONEY MAKES THE
WORLD GO 'ROUND

HOW TO BEAT THE MARKET
WITHOUT UNDERSTANDING
THE FIRST THING ABOUT IT

LESTER WERTHEIMER

MONEY MAKES THE WORLD GO 'ROUND

Copyright © 2015 Lester Wertheimer.

All rights reserved. No part of this book may be used or reproduced by any means, graphic, electronic, or mechanical, including photocopying, recording, taping or by any information storage retrieval system without the written permission of the author except in the case of brief quotations embodied in critical articles and reviews.

The information, ideas, and suggestions in this book are not intended to render professional advice. Before following any suggestions contained in this book, you should consult your personal accountant or other financial advisor. Neither the author nor the publisher shall be liable or responsible for any loss or damage allegedly arising as a consequence of your use or application of any information or suggestions in this book.

iUniverse books may be ordered through booksellers or by contacting:

iUniverse
1663 Liberty Drive
Bloomington, IN 47403
www.iuniverse.com
1-800-Authors (1-800-288-4677)

Because of the dynamic nature of the Internet, any web addresses or links contained in this book may have changed since publication and may no longer be valid. The views expressed in this work are solely those of the author and do not necessarily reflect the views of the publisher, and the publisher hereby disclaims any responsibility for them.

Any people depicted in stock imagery provided by Thinkstock are models, and such images are being used for illustrative purposes only. Certain stock imagery © Thinkstock.

ISBN: 978-1-4917-7340-6 (sc)
ISBN: 978-1-4917-7341-3 (e)

Library of Congress Control Number: 2015911953

Print information available on the last page.

iUniverse rev. date: 08/24/2015

For our children and their children,
who now realize an eternal truth:
Money does not grow on trees.

CONTENTS

INTRODUCTION

The most beautiful words in the
English language are not, "I love you,"
but, "check enclosed."
Dorothy Parker

Imagine for a moment that your Uncle Charlie just died. How sad! A wonderful guy who lived a rich and full life, Uncle Charlie was married and divorced twice, but had no children. His brother–your father–passed away last year, making you his only living relative.

Uncle Charlie's modest apartment featured his most prized possession–a colorful painting of two lovers floating in space by Marc Chagall, which he purchased in Paris years earlier. As far as you know, he had little more of value. That's why you're in total shock to learn that Uncle Charlie was wealthy. His lawyer says that after bills are paid and the estate is settled you will inherit four million dollars. This is so incredibly surreal you can hardly believe it. Honest to God–four million dollars! Yesterday you were barely middle class; today you're a multi-millionaire.

How on earth did Uncle Charlie amass such a fortune on his modest Associate Professor's salary? He always said, "Take care of your money when you're young, kid, and it'll take care of you when you're old." Apparently, he practiced what he preached. The lawyer explained that Uncle Charlie began investing years ago when he was a teaching assistant.

"Every year, without fail, he invested ten percent of his earnings in blue chip stocks that paid dividends. He did that through good times and bad. I don't think he even knew or cared whether the market was up or down; he just kept investing like a robot. And, as far as I know, he never sold a single share of stock. Uncle Charlie apparently realized that simple, steady investing leads to success in the long run."

Now what? You've got Uncle Charlie looking over your shoulder. He's saying, "Be smart, kid; think about your next move. What are you going to do with your money?"

And that's what this short book is about–what is *your* next move, and what are *you* going to do with *your* money? A life-changing fortune is unlikely to fall into your lap, but if you have more money right now than you absolutely need to live, you definitely should think about your next move. How do you handle excess money and what strategies will produce the greatest success without creating more anxiety than profit?

Most investment advice is terrifying. Experts emphasize the hazards–the likelihood of your losing money and the lifetime of regret you'll inevitably suffer by ignoring their advice. They paint a depressing picture of growing old, outliving your money, and being unable to pay your bills. There's little doubt, they insist, you'll end up destitute, if not literally homeless and hungry. Why? Because you're naïve, inexperienced, and you know nothing about investing. Maybe that's true, but why do so many advisors talk down to clients like they're unruly six-year-olds?

Most people are much smarter about money than they realize. They make solid financial decisions based on innate good sense, not because they have a degree in economics. On the other hand, Will Rogers once warned, "You must guard against spending money you don't have on things you don't need to impress people you don't like." That, too, happens occasionally; such as when that insensitive guy next door embellished his front lawn with a phony flock of pink flamingos meant to dazzle the neighborhood. Instead, it irritated every passerby and generated endless hostility from neighbors.

> *People are smarter about money than they realize.*

This book is titled *Money Makes the World Go 'Round*, which means that in today's society money has become more important than ever. But really, how important is it? While some believe money is nearly as essential as oxygen, others think family and health are more important. All agree, however, that living without money would be difficult, if not impossible. Money provides access to every necessity in life, and every necessity has its price.

If you have plenty of money you are indeed blessed. Most people are not that fortunate; they have just about enough to lead a modest life. You should realize that being educated is essential. According to the U.S. Department of Education those with a bachelor's degree earn two-thirds more than those with a high school diploma. And if you pursue a career you love, greater success usually follows. Finally, you must learn to save, invest, and spend wisely.

The subtitle of this book, *How to Beat the Market...* suggests that your investment results may surpass those of the popular averages. Most advisors are unable to do so, and economists insist that—over an extended period—neither can anyone else beat the market. They say that fees, taxes, and human emotions make it nearly impossible for your gains to exceed those of the market indexes. They say those who win are lucky, not skilled. Nevertheless, some people do beat the market, and whether it's skill, luck, or taking uncommon risks, it definitely can be done.

You should know that I am not a financial expert; my training and livelihood is in architecture. Nevertheless, I have frequently beaten the market over past decades by investing in ways described in the chapters that follow.

Some may wonder why I dare offer advice to others on a subject so totally unrelated to my own profession. The simple answer is that years of investment experience have led to the evolution of methods suggested in this book. As a result I have not only earned far more money from my investments than from architecture, but in so doing I have beaten the accomplishments of most financial professionals more times than not.

Believe me, it wasn't always that way. I was forced to face my financial future shortly after completing my architectural education at the University of California in Berkeley. During those arduous years spent over the drawing board it became clear that those of us drawn to this noble art faced a satisfying, but decidedly low-paying, future. In fact, a professor in one of our introductory courses declared that, "Being an architect is similar to being a priest; the rewards, you will find, are mostly spiritual."

What we needed, suggested a fellow student, was an additional source of income independent of our professional practice. "A paper-bag machine!" he said. "A machine that will crank out paper bags 24 hours a day, every day, while we work, sleep, and enjoy our creative lives. The magic machine's products will pay the bills, and without the pressure of scratching out a living, life will become the proverbial bowl of cherries."

A couple of years later two former classmates and I abandoned the paper-bag idea, having discovered the prohibitive cost of purchasing such a device. Instead, we found a challenging piece of property on which we planned to design and build a spec house that would represent the first rung on the ladder to our hypothetical fortune.

We began our venture by creating a program and sketching preliminary designs. Four months later we were still quarreling over the design. Three talented architects were experiencing massive creative differences. Two months later we agreed that friendship was more important than fortune. We dissolved the partnership and put the lot up for sale. A month later a buyer appeared and purchased the land for an amount fifty percent greater than our investment. Our celebration lasted a full week after the close of escrow. I now became a typically overconfident, novice investor. I truly believed I was smarter than I actually was.

A graphic designer, who rented an adjacent space in my office building, was responsible for my next financial adventure. He suggested I meet an acquaintance of his—a Texas oilman named Bobby Ray Wolford. The oilman had come to town to promote shares of oil leases he owned in Oklahoma. The person who showed up was a cliché straight out of central casting—ten-gallon hat, leather-fringed vest, boots, and spurs! I'm not kidding—spurs!

"Where'd you park your horse?" I asked.

"In the garage downstairs," he answered without the hint of a smile.

Bobby Ray proceeded to educate me on the essentials of the oil business, as well as warn me of the incredible regret I'd suffer if I didn't invest in his company. Now, I didn't just fall off the turnip truck, and even at that young age I was an incipient skeptic. But there was something about this six-and-a-half-foot-tall Texan that absolutely charmed me. I ended up buying a single share of a well.

During the next several weeks I received regular, detailed reports and geologic information on the drilling progress. Two months later we struck oil, and I was totally convinced I was an investment virtuoso, if not an absolute genius. Distribution checks appeared regularly, and after four months I had recovered about a third of my original investment.

Then came the pail of cold water. Checks became smaller and three months later they stopped altogether. What happened? Our oil was like the time remaining to a prisoner on death row—it eventually ran out. My now former partner explained, "No one's ever been lowered head-first down one of them holes, so no one knows for sure what's down there. Ah reckon that's the way the good Lord planned it."

Apparently, the good Lord also planned for me to lose half my investment forever, along with considerable confidence in my judgment.

As my adventure in the oil business ended with a pitiful thud I was now free to pursue my fortune elsewhere. The stock market had always interested me, so I began to read every book available on the subject. I even took a course in charting, deemed by many a form of black magic. I read the daily financial pages and was soon ready to take the plunge. Being a bit cautious I invested in the Small Dogs of the Dow (about which you will read later). After one year I was stunned to have made a forty-two percent return on my investment.

Beginner's luck? Absolutely! I've never done that well since, and it is unlikely to ever happen again. It did, however, convince me that money could be made in the market if one is careful and the planets are properly aligned.

The same was not true, however, during the Great Inflation of the 1970s. That was a period when questionable government policies led to record high interest rates, low growth, inflation, high unemployment, and finally, recession. It was a perfect storm resulting in a forty percent decline in the stock market.

During this bleak period I was strongly advised by a financial professional to invest in the safety of bonds. Whereas stocks represent ownership in a company, bonds represent borrowed money that a company repays, with interest, several years down the road. While market forces directly affect those who hold stocks, bondholders are more affected by interest rates. When interest rates rise, bond prices fall. Boy, do they ever!

So you can well imagine what happened to my bonds when the interest rate eventually rose to an astounding 20 percent. My bonds went so far south so quickly I was waving *buenos dias* to people in Tierra del Fuego–on my way to the South Pole–before realizing I was nearly bankrupt. My loss in the "safety" of bonds was considerably greater than any stock loss I've *ever* experienced. And that is what happens when dubious professional advice meets equal parts of blind faith.

I have remained an active investor since those initial experiences, and the lessons learned helped avoid similar disasters. In fact, while pursuing my architectural career I never stopped searching for the preferred path to investment success. Up to a point I've been lucky, but having ridden out several booms and busts, I now believe I've learned to navigate the white waters of the turbulent markets.

Proof of my success led me some years ago to the "safe zone", a term coined by a successful friend who reached a point in life where he no longer worried about money. "I'm in the safe zone now," he declared, "and even if I live to the age of 125, my kids will still inherit enough to be comfortable for the rest of their lives."

Finally, let me tell you an illustrative story about an architectural hero and his encounter with skeptical clients.

Frank Lloyd Wright, the great American architect, was interviewed prior to creating his famous Guggenheim Museum on New York's 5th Avenue. He was asked, "Why should we trust you, Mr. Wright, to create a major museum on a prominent New York avenue when you've never before designed a single museum?"

The confident architect replied, "Having never before designed a single museum is—in fact—my greatest justification and overwhelming advantage."

So by the same reasoning, let us approach investing from a different perspective and attempt to increase our wealth. It might very well end up being as successful an effort as the Guggenheim in New York.

1

IT'S GOOD TO
HAVE MONEY

It is said that the poor are poor
because they haven't enough money.

Anonymous

"Rich or poor," my mother was fond of saying, "it's good to have money." She certainly knew what she was talking about, having come of age during the Great Depression of the 1930s. Those were the days when nobody had enough money. Wealthy businessmen watched their investments plunge, and tragically, some followed them right out the window. Meanwhile, the average John Doe was scraping enough together to feed his family. Industrial production, wholesale prices, and workers wages dropped like one ton of bricks after another as U.S. unemployment rose to a record 25 percent. Banks failed, millions became homeless, and bread lines sprang up everywhere. Except for vocalists and tap dancers in Hollywood musicals, most people were as depressed as the economy.

One afternoon our downstairs neighbor, Mrs. Kaplan, came to our door in tears. "They've shut off our power," she said. "We can't pay our bill. I don't mind using candles at night, but our daughter, Belle, (a misnomer, if there ever was one) can't listen to Little Orphan Annie. Do you mind if she listens on your radio?"

After a few "Annie" episodes, my father paid the Kaplan's electric bill (he called it a loan); Belle's father soon found a job selling shoes, and things quickly returned to normal. My mother needed no further proof; for the rest of her life she was absolutely convinced, "it's good to have money".

Throughout history people have struggled for money, cheated for it, lied and even died for it. Why? Because money can be exchanged for almost everything else in the world. Besides its tangible benefits, money buys freedom, power, respect, and peace of mind. Some believe money can buy everything but happiness. But as Groucho Marx once said, "That may be true, but money lets you choose a better class of misery."

Rich *and* poor want more money these days, and they go about it in a variety of ways. Some look for a better job that pays more, but in a weak economy better jobs may be harder to find than an honest politician. Others wait for a wealthy relative to die, but that takes patience and perhaps wishful thinking—the kind of thinking that leads to a lifetime of guilt.

Then there's the Bonnie and Clyde approach, where you take a direct path to greater wealth by robbing banks. "Why not?" Willie Sutton famously declared, "That's where the money is." Finally, there is the relatively conventional idea of investing your money and hoping for a reasonable return over time. Pretty dull stuff, you might think, but more times than not it works wonders.

Investing takes money, and for some, saving enough to invest is an overwhelming hurdle. The reason people can't save is because they spend more than they earn. It's no surprise; just look at how businesses tempt customers with endless sales, low-interest purchase plans, and buy-one-get-one-free offers. You may not actually need the latest iPhone or a larger television set, but you're obliged to do your part in the interest of maintaining a vigorous economy. It's practically your duty to overspend. Some believe it's the most patriotic thing you can do. Of course you know better, but fiscal discipline in today's society has little more chance than you winning the lottery; and trust me on this one—that's *never* going to happen.

The savings rate in the U.S. these days is truly pathetic. According to the U.S. Commerce Department half of all Americans have no retirement account beyond the promise of Social Security. Those depending solely on that federal program are in for a shock, because the current Social Security benefit averages $1300 per month; that's $15,600 a year. If you are single without any other income you might avoid paying income tax, but you still have the expense of rent, utilities, food, health care, transportation, and—if you can afford a TV—cable service.

You are now dangerously close to the national poverty level, and don't kid yourself; you're in serious financial trouble. If you quit spending right now you could probably celebrate twice a month with a splendid dinner featuring a Big Mac, medium fries, and a large Coke. How about a trip to Disneyland, a new pair of shoes, or an occasional movie? With all due sympathy, you might have thought about that when you were buying a new video game, instead of thinking about your future.

A study by Moody Analytics shows that U.S. adults under the age of thirty-five spend two percent more than they earn. And where does that two percent come from? Anyone with a credit card balance can answer that one. The money is borrowed from the financial institution that issued the credit card. The amount you owe is repaid monthly—with added interest of about fifteen percent—until the balance disappears, which often takes years. If there is a worse way to borrow money than on a credit card, it probably involves someone named Tony the Weasel, who will threaten to break your arm if you miss a payment. Credit card interest may cause similar discomfort, but dealing with a conventional bank is probably better for your long-term health.

Earlier generations were not much thriftier than today's, but this generation differs by having little confidence in investing. People under the age of thirty seem frightened by the stock market. Only twenty-five percent own stocks compared with nearly sixty percent of those over fifty. Many, of course, carry staggering student loan debt; but the major reasons they ignore the market is financial illiteracy and lack of interest.

Young people fail to realize that time is on their side. They can endure market declines and other setbacks, they can afford to take the long view, and they have the magic of compounding working in their favor. The markets are practically made for the young, most of whom ignore those unique advantages.

If you are in your thirties or older and still living with your parents or–worse yet–in a cardboard box on the street, you should realize it's never too late. It is still possible to turn your life around and mend your ways. But first, you must spend less than you earn. That should be everyone's goal, and when you do that, you will suddenly be an investor. Having unspent

> *The goal is to spend less than you earn.*

money, whether or not you realize it, puts you in the

investor class. Yes, it really is that simple. Choosing to put $50 into a bank account represents your first investment decision. Bravo! You're on your way.

The purpose of all investments is to store excess purchasing power for future use, and there are several ways to do that. Perhaps you've already dabbled in one or more of the following options.

The Mattress

Years ago family fortunes were squirreled away in a mattress, cookie jar, or even a hollowed-out book on a shelf near the toilet. (Thieves *never* search for money in a bathroom.) The advantage was its immediate availability and safety, provided the home had a foolproof security system. But this method is risky and makes little sense today. Loss can occur through burglary or fire, or over time, through normal, predictable inflation.

Savings Accounts

A bank or savings association will pay you interest on your deposit, while you and your money enjoy the safety of being federally insured. There is considerable peace of mind knowing that your funds can be withdrawn–with accrued interest–when the deposit term ends. But the miserly rate of earned interest will not make you wealthy anytime soon.

Real Estate

Great fortunes have been made in real estate, but often at considerable risk. When demand exceeds supply you will definitely do well, but when the situation reverses itself property values can fall precipitously. In that event you can either take a loss or be forced to hold on–while mortgage payments and maintenance costs continue–until the real estate market recovers. Eventually it will recover, of course, at about the time you're done tearing out your hair.

Real property generally appreciates at the rate of inflation or better and often includes unique tax advantages. The prime disadvantage is that you may not be able to sell when you need the money. There is also a question of the property's value, which can be a contentious issue between buyer and seller.

Collecting

For those with the knowledge and interest, profitable investments can be made in art, postage stamps, precious gems, antique autos, and even Woody Woodpecker lunch boxes. Those who follow such a consuming interest, however, may be reluctant to sell the Picasso lithograph off the wall when times get tough. Impressive art collections have been sold at enormous profit, but that rarely happens before the collector has gone off to the great art gallery in the sky. Other risks are being assured that what you collect will appeal to someone else, finding a buyer when you need one, and determining a fair market price.

Stock Market

Compared with the alternatives, the stock market offers several unique advantages. Investment is easy, fast, and requires relatively little capital to begin. The markets operate continuously, so there are always buyers and sellers for a listed stock or mutual fund. You are assured absolute liquidity, which means you can sell your investments for cash by a phone call or one quick click of a computer key. And the fair market price is determined by thousands of buyers and sellers on the open market. No other investment matches the stock market for convenience and opportunity.

Many potential investors consider investing to be as incomprehensible as the scientific theory of teleportation.

"Why must it be so complicated?" asks the neophyte. "I know nothing about stocks and haven't the faintest idea where to begin. How on earth do you expect me to pick winners among 5000 companies or 20,000 mutual funds?"

The choices do indeed boggle the mind. And the incredible amount of free advice adds further confusion. Who do you listen to? Who can you trust? Is it possible the market newsletter you're reading isn't worth your time or even the paper it's printed on? And how about your advisor, who's beginning to resemble a friendly riverboat gambler? Is he aiming to get his greedy hands on your hard-earned savings?

New investors often fear that markets are like gaming casinos, where the house always wins. In fact, the stock market has been referred to as "The Other Las Vegas". But is that a fair comparison? In Las Vegas all the odds are with the house. You might win a jackpot now and then, but if you continue to gamble the casino will win and you will lose. That's not only a fact of life; it's how casinos remain profitable. The odds overwhelmingly favor them over the poor blackjack player, sitting patiently, night after night, praying for a king and an ace.

The markets, on the other hand, favor the investor; all the odds are with *you*. Just look at a chart of the Dow Jones Industrial Average (next page), and you will see a line that wiggles upward over the past one hundred years, from about 50 to over 18,000. That means the most widely followed measure of the market has appreciated during the past one hundred years by over 36,000 percent! You would never get anywhere near that return in Las Vegas–not even in your wildest dreams.

An interesting example of the market's enduring power can be found in one of the Dow Jones Industrial Average components–Coca-Cola, a company founded in 1886 by

100-Year Trend

Dow Jones Industrial Average

WITH APPROXIMATE VALUES INDICATED AT 25-YEAR INTERVALS

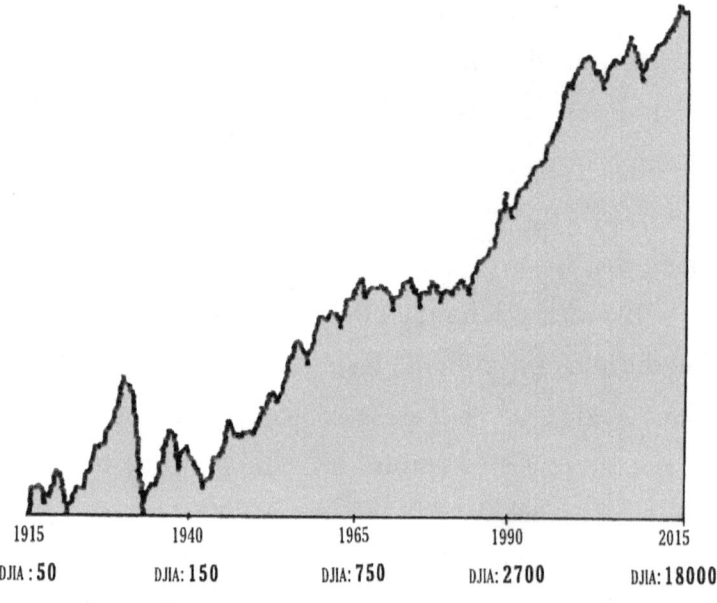

1915	1940	1965	1990	2015
DJIA : 50	DJIA: 150	DJIA: 750	DJIA: 2700	DJIA: 18000

READERS SHOULD NOTE THE CONSISTENT DIRECTION OF THIS CHART.

IT IS UP!

AS WE EXPECT YOUR INVESTMENT RESULTS WILL BE.

Colonel John Pemberton. The Colonel was wounded in the Civil War, became addicted to morphine, and sought a substitute for the dangerous opiate. The ingredients of his original recipe were cocaine, derived from the coca leaf, and caffeine from the kola nut. Put them together, change the "k" of kola to "c" and, *voila*, you have Coca-Cola. The original syrup was sold to pharmacists, who mixed it with soda water and sold it for a nickel a glass as a dietary supplement for upset stomachs.

The company was sold in 1919 and went public on the New York Stock Exchange at $40 a share. Now here's the mind-blowing part of the story: If you purchased a single share of Coca-Cola in 1919, held the stock through a dozen stock splits and reinvested the dividends each year, by 2012 you would own more than 9000 shares worth nearly $1,750,000! What's more, the income you would receive from dividends, that year alone, would have been $22,000.

Now clearly, if you were old enough in 1919 to buy that original share of Coke, you are probably dead; but you have to appreciate the amazing power of compounded dividends, together with the patience it would take to hold a stock for more than ninety years.

The point is simply this: The value of good companies that pay dividends is eventually recognized by investors and over time will generate astounding results–exactly like Uncle Charlie's amazing legacy.

If the markets appreciate most of the time–and they do–why, you may ask, do so many investors complain about market losses? Some years ago the writer, Bill Adler, collected dozens of letters written by disillusioned investors to their financial advisors. The book was titled *Letters to Wall Street* and a sample of these follow:

Gentlemen:
Could you please recommend some stocks that will go up? I have plenty of the other kind.
Truly yours,
Larry G. – New York City

Dear Mr. Gross:
My wife says that if I continue to lose money in the market she is going to leave me. Keep up the good work.
Yours sincerely,
Bruce R. – Pittsburgh

Dear Mr. Allen:
Since you have been handling my account for the past three years I have been buying high and selling low. Is there any chance this trend might be reversed anytime soon?
Respectfully,
Elaine W. – Wheeling, West Virginia

Gentlemen:
Should a person invest in the market for pleasure or profit? The reason I ask is because, so far, I've achieved neither.
Peter W. – Baltimore

Yes, the letters are amusing, but the dissatisfaction and pain of loss is clearly apparent. The important question is this: How does one avoid becoming the next Peter W. from Baltimore who derived neither pleasure nor profit from his investment experience? Do you simply ignore financial markets and conclude this is not for you? Or do you engage in a concentrated study of the markets, which is encouraged by most financial guidebooks?

In my opinion neither choice is necessary or advisable. No investor should be discouraged from studying the markets, the economy, or the entire world of economics, if he or she so chooses. But I believe that is unwarranted, and for many it would lead to one massive migraine after another.

Many consider the bewildering world of finance to be so painful they will do anything to avoid the experience. That is why their solution is to hire a professional and throw the whole mess into someone else's lap.

The markets can be intimidating, and hiring an investment advisor for guidance is understandable. But those who allow a professional to buy and sell in their name, and make investment decision with little client contact, are playing a dangerous game. Abdicating responsibility for your assets is a genuine invitation to disaster. Assuming your advisor is as morally pure as freshly driven snow, you can still get into trouble if he or she acts more conservatively than Calvin Coolidge, the most conservative president who ever lived, or as wildly adventurous as Blackbeard, flying his skull and crossbones on the high seas.

Worse yet, many investment pros fail to give their clients the best advice on the goods they offer. Instead, they often recommend products that will generate the highest commissions. Remember this: No one cares as much about your money as you. Really, they don't. And despite their impeccable credentials, advisors are only human. If they were right most of the time they wouldn't need you or any other client for that matter. They would simply buy what they're selling and relax until their ship comes in.

> *No one cares as much about your money as you.*

2014 was a near disaster for financial advisors and investment experts. This was not the first time this happened, but the year was notable for the number of active, stock-picking managers who got trounced, relative to the market, with their worst performance in decades. They were universally wrong on stock prices, bond prices, interest rates, rate of inflation, and price of oil. If there is anything here to be learned it is that market forecasting has its limits, and the future is truly unknowable. That is why one should not act on all the available advice, but rather select a safer option for getting rich slowly but surely.

It is not always obvious to beginning, starry-eyed investors that markets move in two directions, up and down; and it is impossible to predict which direction they will go on any given day. On most days the market will go up. Why? Because over the long term markets have always gone up. Take another look at the long-term chart of the Dow Jones Industrial average; its direction is undeniably upward. Over the same span of time everything else has also gone up. Inflation is a fact of economic life, and the cost of nearly everything has consistently risen over the years.

You should also know that the ups and downs of the markets often exceed the most rational expectations, especially the downs, which move at a more accelerated pace. At times they appear to be aided by the sheer force of gravity. There is also the matter of investor's emotional instability–if not outright hysteria–that cause prices to go up or down into uncharted ecospheres. It has been said that the market will do whatever it must to confound the greatest number of people, and that includes rising and falling to outrageous levels.

Predicting the movement of the market is impossible and hardly worth one's time. Expert predictions generally range from euphoric to dismal, as might be expected in a free market. If everyone wanted to buy, for example, there would be no market; there must be sellers as well as buyers for markets to exist. Thus, the endless advice available often ranges all over the place. If you try to follow every market guru you will soon become dizzy, and eventually, a professional cynic.

My first broker many years ago was a diamond in the rough by the name of Art Altschuler, who used to say, "Anyone in this cockamamie business is happy to sell you an investment, but they have no idea if they're selling you a passport to happiness or a worthless piece of garbage. So do your own homework, and take all suggestions—including those from me—with a grain of salt."

So what's an investor to do? To begin with, if you want to get rich quick, rob a bank, the stock market is not for you. But if you want to get rich slowly but surely, read on. The answer to your question will likely be revealed in subsequent chapters.

2

RULES OF THE ROAD

That money talks, I'll not deny.

I had it once, it said, "Goodbye".

Richard Armour

Rules establish the principles and standards by which we live. They guide human activity by telling us what is socially acceptable, and as such, they are the basis of a civilized society. An absence of rules leads to confusion, chaos, and lawlessness. Imagine the result if people suddenly ignored the white line down the middle of a road or disregarded red traffic lights. The result would be utter pandemonium.

Since the beginning of time societies have operated by rules favoring the majority of people within each society. There were standards of conduct long before Moses returned from Mount Sinai with God's Ten Commandments, but with that legendary event laws were literally chiseled in stone. The Commandments dealt with unethical behavior that—we can only assume—was completely out of control. As a result, new prohibitions were declared against lying, stealing, adultery, murder, and coveting your neighbor's house, wife, servant, and ox—pretty much the same sort of unsavory pursuits that goes on today, except that coveting a neighbor's ox these days is fairly rare.

On the other hand, antisocial behavior has changed little since the time of Moses. We may believe that modern society is more ethical than ancient societies, but there is little evidence to support that view. A quick glance at the daily news reveals a steady stream of remarkably corrupt conduct. Politicians are routinely accused of wrongdoing, overzealous policemen often abuse their power, and there are endless burglaries, murders, rapes, and drive-by shootings.

Though we remain a predominately religious nation, the ethical basis of every major religion, "Do unto others…" is consistently ignored. Worse yet, we

> *Religious ethics have been ignored for years.*

have been at war almost continuously since the end of World War II, and political hawks remain eager to drop the next bomb.

Markets do not deal with matters as serious as war or murder. However, some guidelines remain valuable lessons for investors who wish to understand market action, while avoiding common investment problems and pitfalls.

Perhaps this is more than you bargained for in a simple book about the market, but a pearl of wisdom might be just the thing to lighten the load when your investments are heading straight for the sewage treatment plant.

Any stock or any fund can do anything at any time without warning or reason.

When an investment soars to incredible heights or plunges to frightening depths do not look for a logical explanation. Often there is none. It is merely the perverse action of buyers and sellers expressing their emotions as they follow each other heavenward or off a cliff. Experts are quick to offer explanations, but days later you may learn that it was merely someone, somewhere, initiating a now discredited rumor.

Investments go up and down because of supply and demand.

When there are more buyers than sellers, investments go up; when there are more sellers, they go down. Supply and demand has controlled the price of things from the beginning of time. If there is something everybody wants, we call it priceless. If nobody wants it, we call it worthless. If you hear that an investment is overvalued or undervalued you should realize that it is the correct value—precisely the value the market has determined through buying and selling. Things do not sell for what someone believes to be a fair price; they sell for what someone is willing to pay.

Cut your losses and let your profits run.

Most market experts agree that this golden rule will do more to improve profits than almost any other bit of advice. Sadly, investments occasionally turn against investors like angry in-laws who never approved of their daughter's choice of husband in the first place. Mistakes happen, and when they do you must limit your loss and move on. Your first loss is your best loss. Hanging on and hoping things will improve is like believing in the Easter bunny once you've passed the age of six. It also leads, quite often, to greater losses; so sell when it becomes clear that success lies elsewhere. If, on the other hand, your investment moves in the right direction, let it run until it exhausts itself. With small losses and large gains, you don't have to be right even half the time.

Beware of those bringing gifts of insider information, rumors, or tips.

The world of finance is overflowing with advice, most of which can be safely ignored. Everybody has a theory, an opinion, and often, an ax to grind. Listen to them all, if you care to, but make up your own mind. You're probably more capable than you think, and besides, most investments require common sense, not a business degree from Harvard. If, on the other hand, you follow someone else's advice, you might just as well hand over your money to that person.

Buy and sell at the market.

Always accept the going price for any investment when buying or selling. Don't wait for it to go up or down another few cents a share. Those who expect to buy at the bottom or sell at the top will likely miss the boat. As the great investor Bernard Baruch once said, "This cannot be done—except by liars".

Following are proverbs that have become part of the investment folklore. Like most legends, each contains an element of truth as well as a heaping spoonful of misconception. Again, these are not laws chiseled in stone; they are merely the collective wisdom of those who learned the hard way.

"Money is the safest investment"

The implication is that while all investments carry a degree of risk, holding cash is relatively risk free.

Unfortunately, this popular belief is deceptive. Money is only good for what it can buy. Since purchasing power is steadily eroded through inflation, holding cash can be less safe than other investments, like, for example, the S&P 500 index, which automatically reflects inflationary pressures. It may be comforting to have an envelope in the top drawer filled with $100 bills, but the comfort quickly fades when the value of each bill becomes $95 perhaps a year later.

"Buy them and put them away"

This makes good sense, generally speaking, because most investments will appreciate very well without your periodic interference. However, there are times when a little supervision is necessary. If, for example you owned Washington Mutual, Enron, or General Motors just before they went bankrupt several years ago you might have lost a fortune. There were warnings, of course, but having put them away you never noticed. Nobody knows the future, and that is why investments can never be safely "put away".

"You cannot go broke taking a profit"

This might have been true for Commodore Vanderbilt, who coined the phrase, but it might not be true for you. Anxious investors may watch uneasily as their investments fluctuate. When they finally move a few dollars above the purchase price they quickly sell. Hooray! They now have a small profit from which they must deduct the commissions for buying and selling. They must also deduct the federal tax due for the short-term capital gain. All too often they discover they didn't make a cent. How did that happen? More small profits, they discover, could eventually add up to a pittance.

"Bulls make money, Bears make money, but Hogs get slaughtered"

A "bull" believes the market will go up, whereas a "bear" believes the market will go down. Both can make money by placing the correct bet and buying long or selling short. Being a "hog", on the other hand, implies that one is driven by greed and avarice that will ultimately be his or her undoing. Actually, if you are invested in a promising situation there is no reason why you shouldn't be a bit hoggish about it, because hogs often do make money. You just better know what you're doing.

"Don't put all your eggs in one basket"

This popular saying advises one to avoid placing all assets into one investment. It's considered much safer to diversify. Many great fortunes have been made, however, by concentration, not diversification. It's known as putting all your eggs in one basket and keeping a sharp eye on the basket.

3

GET A GRIP

The investor's chief problem
—and even worse enemy—
is likely to be himself.
Benjamin Graham

It is a sad fact that most people in our country are overweight—nearly 70 percent, according to the U.S. Center for Disease Control. And among those, half are considered obese. Many overweight people rationalize their condition with a variety of quasi-medical excuses, such as their quirky metabolism, unfortunate heredity, or their abnormal skeletal framework. Apparently any explanation will do, except this one: "I have no willpower, none at all, and I eat too much. Sad but true; that's just the way it is."

Delusional thinking is never helpful, not when it leads to overeating and certainly not when it involves money. That is why well-adjusted people are better investors than those who are not. Of course, well-adjusted people are usually better at everything. We all have an annoying assortment of neuroses that prevent us from doing our best, but when it comes to financial dealings those eccentricities can be costly.

The first thing you must realize is that investing is not a matter of life or death. Nobody enjoys losing money, but when financial setbacks happen–and they do–it need not be a death knell. You must have the ability to identify and overcome the psychological weaknesses that get people into trouble with their investments. If you can recognize this behavior beforehand, you may avoid tripping over your own feet, which often leads to financial decisions contrary to your best interests. Some of the more significant emotional qualities follow.

Overconfidence

Overconfidence refers to believing you are smarter or more capable than you really are. It leads 90 percent of people to claim they are above average drivers. Also, when people declare they are 90 percent certain of something, studies show they are right about 70 percent of the time. Overconfidence bias leads people to believe they can be successful active investors, when in fact; many of them should be buying index funds.

Selective Memory

Overconfident behavior often leads to selective memory, which is our way of forgetting painful experiences. We certainly don't want to remember ignoring Apple stock at $30 a share or buying Enron just before it went bankrupt. Such memories threaten our self-image and make us doubt our investing ability. So we tend to forget or, worse yet, deny those events ever happened. As Mark Twain once said, "Denial isn't just a river in Egypt."

Loss Aversion

Loss aversion is the reluctance of people to sell a losing investment. Investors are more willing to sell winning positions in order to take some profits, while avoiding the embarrassment of taking a loss in a losing position. That is why some investors hold a losing investment long after it becomes apparent it's going nowhere but south. "When it gets back to where I bought it," they say, "I'll reconsider." Sadly, their purchase price is now a totally arbitrary figure that the investment may not reach for another decade or two.

Crowd Psychology

People are social creatures, and in the absence of information they tend to follow the crowd. Behavioral scientists claim that a crowd becomes a sort of single person endowed with the brains of its lowest member and led by the loudest one choosing to lead. Benjamin Graham, the father of value investing, once said, "You are neither right nor wrong because the crowd disagrees with you".

Wishful Thinking

Demosthenes, the ancient Greek statesman, said, "What a man wishes, so shall he believe." In other words, people see what they want to see. If the market is in a prolonged decline some investors will rationalize the movement as "Not that bad; it could be worse". They will watch patiently as their investments plunge to new depths, and they will sit calmly and silently while they figuratively bleed to death.

The same sort of delusion is detected when gamblers roll dice. If they want a high number they roll the dice vigorously, and if they want a lower number, they roll them gently. It is often pleasant to ignore reality, but it won't add a single cent to your bank account.

Other Negative Emotions

There are a great many negative emotions, all quite human, that hinder investment success.

Rationalization, for example, allows you to create a reason for what's happening, but prevents you from accepting the facts as they appear.

Greed is the reluctance to sell an investment when it reaches unrealistic heights. Even though investors know "a tree does not grow to the sky", they continue to hold on for the last few dollars.

Fear of losing money is one of the most powerful market forces in both up and down markets. They say a winning market climbs a wall of worry, and a plunging market magnifies the terror.

Envy rears its head when you hear of someone who just made a killing in the market. You decide to chase the same investment, but sadly, that ship has sailed.

Guilt is the feeling that you simply don't deserve to make money. Like compulsive gamblers, even when the investor wins, he is bound to keep playing until he loses.

Positive Emotions

The emotions that encourage successful investing are less common, but they are qualities to which all should aspire.

Objectivity implies basing decisions on facts, not guesses, not suppositions, and not wishful thinking.

Patience is generally rewarded in both up and down markets. You must not rush into a purchase or a sale, and especially must not act out of boredom.

Flexibility means you must give up a rigid strategy when it stops working. When all goes against you it is time to consider plan B.

Common Sense as they say is "uncommon", but good judgment will produce better results than almost any other human quality. Common sense means trusting your judgment and ignoring the chaos of those charging into an investment or throwing their stocks out the window. You know more than you think. Trust yourself.

Optimism in the market produces better results than pessimism. Since the markets historically rise, optimists are usually winners.

A Sense of Humor, finally, is an absolute necessity. As I said earlier, this is not a matter of life or death, so enjoy your profits, become wiser from your losses, and remember, there's more to life than chasing money. As the Sammy Cahn lyrics advise:

It's only money; it's only dough,
And the people who crave it,
who worship and save it,
All come to know
You can't take it with you
when you go.

4

BASIC STRATEGIES

Take your savings and buy some good stock;

hold it till it goes up, then sell it.

If it don't go up, don't buy it."

Will Rogers

The subtitle of this book suggests you can be successful and *beat the market without understanding the first thing about it.* That is not only true, but it has little to do with luck, karma, or any extraterrestrial interference. It doesn't matter whether you know the difference between a stock and a bond or are able to decipher an annual report. If you employ the common sense strategies that follow you will make money and do well over the long term.

The following strategies assume you know nothing about the stock market and may not have the time or inclination to learn more. It doesn't really matter. These proposals are essentially mechanical formulas for beating the market, and they do not require anything more than following directions, which—I assure you—are simpler than putting together a bookcase from IKEA.

The first of these strategies involves purchasing an index fund composed of the common stocks that make up the Standard and Poor's 500 average. Many investment companies offer such funds, and their differences are slight. The idea here is that your investment results will never be worse than the general market. Of course, your profits will never exceed those of the market either. However, your results will exceed those of more than sixty percent of stock picking professionals. That's right, without knowing—or even caring—what stocks you actually hold, you will beat well over half of the professionals at their own game. And you will do this at a fraction of the average fees professionals generally charge. This is the perfect vehicle for those who want to get rich slowly and with the fewest number of cardiac disturbances.

The Standard and Poor's strategy is about as easy as investing gets. But the next strategy, Dogs of the Dow, is nearly as easy and has the advantage of generally beating stock market indexes. Portfolio manager, Michael O'Higgins, discovered years ago that purchasing the ten highest yielding of the thirty Dow Industrial stocks and holding them for one year produced exceptional results. The outcome was even better for what are called the Small Dogs, the five lowest price stocks among the ten highest yielding.

The entire process seems much too easy, but the Dogs have beaten the market averages for most of the past forty years, and sometimes by a considerable margin. You don't even have to figure out which are the current Dogs, as the website, *dogsofthedow.com* updates this information each day. Simply click on *Current Doggishness*, and the information will readily appear.

The final strategy is a bit more complicated than the previous two, but the rewards can be substantially greater. This strategy combines momentum investing in mutual funds with regular upgrading. Momentum investing requires you to purchase mutual funds that have appreciated the most within a reasonable time span.

And this requires you to actually follow the progress of funds to determine which are performing best. This information is easily available online, so time spent in research is not particularly demanding. Though this strategy will work with any group of mutual funds, the best results are frequently obtained by concentrating on sector funds, those that specialize in a specific investment area, such as Healthcare, Transportation, or Electronics. By regularly tracking the results of these funds you will discover which are rising and which are lagging. When one of your funds is lagging and another appears to be rising, you simply trade the laggard for the riser.

You will notice that none of these strategies require you to choose individual stocks. Even specific stocks in the Dogs of the Dow are determined by a strict formula, not by you. The reason you should not pick individual stocks is because it is nearly impossible to do so consistently or profitably. The most talented portfolio managers spend a lifetime determining which stocks to purchase, and most often they are unable to outperform the Standard & Poor's 500 Index. Why then would you think you could do better than the professionals?

Most brokerage houses, as well as other advisory services, publish lists of suggested stocks for you to purchase. These ideas, generated by their research departments, produce a steady stream of recommendations as regularly as TV writers create episodes for soap operas.

"Our stock of the week", announces one service; *"Our investment idea of the month"*, says another. You should understand that great investment ideas do not appear on schedule, like supermarket specials during a holiday weekend. They appear when something exceptional happens to make a company's stock particularly attractive. There are times when no stock is especially attractive, but regardless, most research departments continue to crank out the latest hot-off-the-press, can't-miss opportunity.

The bottom line is this: Ignore the noise of advisors selling "the must-buy stock of the moment", and stick with the proven formula plans that follow. You won't always win either way, but the odds favor those who follow a logical, disciplined approach.

5

THE S&P 500 STRATEGY

Money is not the root of all evil,

lack of money is.

Mark Twain

One of the most comprehensive measures of stock market performance is Standard and Poor's weighted index of the 500 large-capitalization, actively traded common stocks. Included in the index are companies like Apple, Johnson & Johnson, Exxon Mobil, Microsoft, and McDonald's; companies that represent every major area of investment, from airlines to utilities. It is regarded as the best single gauge of the country's foremost companies in leading industries.

The Standard and Poor's Corporation combined Henry Poor's 1868 Manual of Railroads with Luther Blake's 1906 Standard Statistics Bureau, which provided financial information on non-railroad companies. For the past seventy-five years the S&P 500 has included a significant portion of the market's total value; thus, it is regarded as an index representing the entire market.

It was John Bogle, founder of the Vanguard Group, who in the 1970s detected the superiority of index funds over traditional, actively managed mutual funds. He contended that stock pickers were simply unable to outperform the general market over the long term; and throughout the past forty or so years, in good markets and bad, he has been right. In all those years fewer than forty percent of actively managed funds have outperformed the S&P 500 index. In other words, the low-cost, non-managed stock index has beaten over sixty percent of active stock pickers!

Better news yet for Bogleheads: In 2014, nearly ninety percent of portfolio managers were trounced by the S&P 500 index. That's right; just about one out of ten was able to beat the unmanaged, low cost index. So why would a rational investor go elsewhere with his or her investment dollars when all the odds for success favor low cost index funds? Or as Bogle maintains, "Why look for a needle in the haystack when you can buy the whole haystack?"

Index funds have advantages over other mutual funds for several practical reasons. First, since index funds contain every stock in the index, fund managers have few decisions to make. The S&P 500 Index, by its very definition, contains the stock of 500 companies making up the average. Thus, managers need not spend time doing research or exploring further investment ideas. Less management activity means lower cost to the fund company; hence, lower cost to you, the investor.

The second advantage of holding 500 stocks means greater diversification, and thus, greater safety. Energy stocks might tank one day, but airlines will then benefit from cheaper fuel costs and appreciate. Or if the economy deteriorates and stocks take a severe dive, gold stocks will generally rise, as investors flock to the security of the yellow metal. There is safety in numbers, and there is no greater diversification than a fund that contains every segment of the market.

Finally, holding the 500 stocks in the S&P index means there is little reason for an investment company to buy or sell stocks, resulting in a minimum of trading. Mutual funds managers frequently sell one stock to buy another, and the turnover ratio of some funds can exceed one hundred percent over the course of a year. Believe it or not, between January and December nearly every one of a portfolio's holdings might be completely different. What that means to investors is that at year's end you might receive an unexpected tax bill from capital gains that will hit you like Hurricane Katrina and cause just as much damage to your financial well-being.

John Bogle argues that low-cost index funds are defined by simplicity and common sense. He insists that paying the added cost for advice, as in a typical mutual fund, is rarely worthwhile, and that superstar fund managers often fail to deliver superstar results. He also advises that one should buy a fund and hold it for

> *The cost of advice is rarely worthwhile.*

the long term. How long? He doesn't say, but one could guess the holding period might approach that of the famous investor, Warren Buffet. When Buffet was asked a similar question about when to sell, he answered, "Never."

Most large financial institutions offer a variety of index funds, but the Vanguard Group has, arguably, the largest selection of funds at the lowest fees. Their sixty or so funds include, beside the S&P 500, a Total Stock Market Index with about 3000 domestic stocks, Total Bond Market Index with about 7000 bonds, and Total International Stock Index with nearly 6000 stocks from companies throughout the world.

There are at least fifty mutual funds and exchange-traded funds (ETFs) that try to match the returns of the S&P 500. The results achieved by these funds are not all the same, largely because their management fees vary considerably. For example, the fees of Fidelity's S&P 500 Index Fund are nearly double Vanguard's, and T. Rowe Price's Equity Index 500 Fund fees are more than five times those of Vanguard's. That is why Vanguard's return in 2014 beat the return of the other two funds by up to one-half a percentage point.

The recent trend is clearly away from fund managers and toward passive investment in index funds. It is not only the superior performance of the index funds, but the enormous saving over the years in management fees. As the merits of passive investments become more recognized financial advisors have begun to recommend low-cost funds to their clients. In so doing some add their own fees on top of the fund's fee, and the investor is hardly aware he or she is paying what is–in essence–a finder's fee. So if you are drawn to such a fund, buy it directly from the investment company that offers the fund.

You should understand that index funds will never beat the market, because index funds *are* the market. They now represent a third of all mutual fund assets, leading some to fear that when everyone believes indexing is a sure bet its advantage cannot possibly last. Detractors say there has never been an easy path to financial success, and that includes the easiest strategy of all–index funds.

Nevertheless, you can reasonably assume that the benefits of passive investment will continue until stock pickers manage to outperform the indexes. Meanwhile, don't hold your breath. Invest your serious dollars with an index fund, and prepare to beat the pros.

6

DOGS OF THE DOW

Money is better than poverty,

if only for financial reasons.

Woody Allen

Do you yearn for a super simple idea for investing? An idea that promises so much it seems it can't possibly work? Welcome to the Dogs of the Dow! A "dog" in Wall Street lingo is defined as an unattractive, underperforming stock that is hardly worth your attention. Even if it pays an above-average dividend, it's not going anywhere anytime soon. So, who wants to own a boring laggard that most others consider about as welcome as a case of measles? Well, if you're looking to earn a superior return on your investment, the answer is *you*.

The Dow Jones Industrial Average (DJIA), of which The Dogs are a part, consists of thirty large, publicly traded U.S. companies that represent the total activity of all industrial stocks. These are generally considered the blue chips of the market. Created in 1896 by Charles Dow and Edward Jones, the DJIA is the most cited and most widely recognized market index. When one asks, "How's the market doing?" the answer always refers to the DJIA.

Components of the average change rarely–usually when certain companies become more representative of current industry. In 1896, the original components included–among others–American Sugar, Chicago Gas, and Tennessee Coal and Iron. Electronics was virtually unknown, so the addition of Microsoft and Intel, almost one hundred years later, recognized that as economic life evolves, so too, do the thirty companies that comprise the Dow Jones Industrial Average.

The Dogs of the Dow, as originally conceived, consisted of the ten DJIA stocks with the highest dividend yields. High yield is a contrarian indicator–a way to spot bargains. It is essentially the same strategy used in value investing. Certain companies (Dogs) may become temporarily out of favor, oversold, and abandoned. But these are solid, blue chip companies; and history reveals that the value of such companies is eventually recognized, at which time they tend to outperform. In other words, "Every dog has its day."

The Dog strategy proposes that an investor buy an equal dollar amount of stocks, hold them for one year, and then rebalance with stocks that are the new highest yielders. By so doing, you are forced to sell stocks that have appreciated the most and, consequently, now yield a smaller dividend. (As a stock price rises its yield goes down.) In addition, you are obliged to buy new stocks with higher yields. Stocks which have gone nowhere, or in which you may have a loss, are usually carried over for another year. Thus, you are forced to buy low and sell high–every investor's dream.

There are several variations of the Dogs of the Dow strategy, and the one with the greatest success– and advised here–is called the Small Dogs. These are the five lowest price companies among the ten highest yielding Dogs of the Dow. The Small Dogs have, over time, outperformed the ten original Dogs of the Dow by a few percentage points. In 2014, for example, while the Big Dogs appreciated nearly eleven percent, the Small Dogs were up six percentage points more. But as investment companies like to warn, *"past performance is no guarantee of future results."*

New investors are encouraged to begin with the Small Dogs, not only because results are likely to be better, but overseeing five stocks is easier than watching ten. Theoretically, there is little need to oversee anything. After purchasing the five stocks you might book a 'round the world voyage and ignore their performance for a full year. As curiosity is a human trait, however, taking a peek periodically is perfectly normal. Incidentally, the holding period of one year recognizes that long-term profits, if any, will be taxed most favorably.

As to the timing of your purchase, the original program suggests you jump in on the first trading day of the year. Many Dog proponents follow that recommendation, which leads to the notion that if you purchased stocks in late December there might conceivably be a positive bump from the rash of purchases that occur on the New Year's first trading day.

Actually, the Dog strategy works equally well despite the day, week, or month of the year stocks are purchased, so long as you hold them for a full year.

It should be pointed out that no investment theory is foolproof or will always result in great success. There have been disappointing years when the Dogs faltered, failed to match the major averages, and even plunged, as in 2008, during the last major recession. However, as the market generally goes up, and because you are

> *No investment theory is foolproof.*

forbidden to tinker with your Dogs for twelve months, chances are your profits will rise as well. After all, you're dealing with solid blue chip companies, you're collecting generous dividends along the way, and as an added bonus, you should be sleeping more soundly through the night.

Though we strongly support the idea of the Small Dogs, some who have experimented with the Dog strategy claim that other variations may be even more beneficial. The Motley Fool is a financial service company founded by brothers David and Tom Gardner. Their motto is to: *Educate, Amuse, and Enrich*, and to a large degree they succeed in all three objectives. The Motley Fool has come up with a Dog formula called the "Foolish Four."

One begins their version with the same ten highest yielding stocks of the DJIA 30 Industrials. You then select the five lowest price stocks, as in the Small Dogs. Toss out the lowest price stock, double your investment in the second lowest price stock, and buy equal dollar shares of the remaining three stocks. You will end up with four stocks; 40 percent invested in the lowest price one and 20 percent in each in the other three.

The Motley Fool insists the Foolish Four will consistently beat the Small Dogs by about four percentage points per year. In fact, during 2014 the Foolish Four topped the Small Dogs by precisely that amount. On the other hand, there have been years when it would have been foolish to invest in the Foolish Four. Once again, be aware that the future is impossible to predict.

An even more complex variation, reported by the Motley Fool, was a suggestion several years ago by Larry Gott, who asked, "Why just the Dow?" He went on to suggest that you consider the Far East and

European markets as well. Known as the "Global 15", the portfolio consisted of the five highest-yielding, lowest-priced stocks from the Hang Seng Index (Hong Kong) and the Financial Times Stock Exchange Index (London), in addition to the Small Dogs.

So, how did that work out? During the twenty-year span computed by the author, he claims the Global 15 beat the Small Dogs by about ten percentage points. It may be a considerable effort to construct such a portfolio, but if you can actually make an increased profit of ten percent it might be worth looking into.

Having had no experience with the Global 15, I suggest that you to tread carefully. My personal preference is to stick with the simpler Dog strategies that take less time and energy. Those who remain intrigued by the idea of the Global 15, however, are advised to follow the system on paper for a month or two before committing real money.

7

MOMENTUM INVESTING

We're in the money,

We're in the money,

We've got a lot of what it takes to get along!

Words & Music by

Al Dubin and Harry Warren

Sir Isaac Newton, the brilliant English mathematician and physicist, conceived his Laws of Motion in the latter half of the seventeenth century. His First Law, the Law of Inertia, originally published in *Principia Mathmatica* in 1687, states:

An object at rest remains at rest, and an object in motion remains in motion with the same speed and in the same direction, unless acted upon by an unbalanced force.

This chapter was not intended to be a migraine-producing science lesson, but investment theory often wanders into unfamiliar areas, so bear with me.

To illustrate the first part of Newton's Law, a book sitting on a table remains at rest, even though the force of gravity is assumed to pull the book downward. We can infer, however, that the book remains at rest because the table pushes the book upward. Thus, two equal and opposite forces balance each other, and the book stays where it is.

The second part of the law states that if a body is set in motion it will keep on moving, with the same velocity and direction, unless an unbalanced force brings it to rest. Experience shows that friction is the ever-present, unbalanced retarding force. Thus, a small stone thrown onto dry pavement will travel a short distance; whereas the same stone thrown onto a frozen lake will travel a much greater distance, since the frictional force on ice is considerably less than on a paved street. If friction could be eliminated entirely, which is virtually impossible, the stone would theoretically continue to move indefinitely, with undiminished velocity, exactly like a spacecraft orbiting the earth.

What Newton's law demonstrates is that without the presence of unbalanced forces, in this case gravity and friction, the natural tendency of objects is to keep on doing what they're doing.

What, you may ask, has this to do with making money in the stock market? Just this: Newton's Law of Inertia may be directly applied to the action of individual stocks and mutual funds. In other words, an advancing stock, or fund of stocks, will continue to advance or decline unless acted upon by an unbalanced force.

In the case of an advancing stock, the unbalanced force that alters its direction may be publication of the company's disappointing earnings or something as grave as the premature death of the company's president. As for a declining stock, the unbalanced force changing its direction might be an increase in the stock's dividend or news of an impending buyout offer.

Unbalanced forces are generally unanticipated and will stop a stock or fund from doing what it has been doing, often with the same force as a seatbelt when you jam on the car's brakes.

The important lesson is this: One should invest in stocks or funds that are going up most dynamically and continue to hold them until they stop going up or can be traded for others that are going up even more dynamically.

Some years ago this strategy was called Trend Investing, and it encouraged one to buy not only stocks going up, but also those making new highs. Stocks making new highs, it was believed, were the ones that

> *Invest in stocks or funds going up.*

would continue to reach even higher highs. That was as commonly true then as it is today.

Investment professionals employ numerous tools to determine which stocks and funds will do best and where the market is heading. There are dozens of indicators, such as short interest ratio, advance-decline lines, breadth of trading, price-earning ratios, and more charts than were carried on sailing vessels since the time of Columbus. Forget all that. All you need to know is what's going up. You don't even care why it's going up, or in fact, what the advancing company produces or if it is profitable. It's going up; that's reason enough to buy it.

This advice may sound unorthodox to some, if not actually sacrilegious. However, regardless of what common sense, popular opinion, or wishful thinking may lead you to believe, the movement of an investment going at supersonic speed will generally continue to advance or decline beyond all common logic. Eventually, at some point, every investment will stop advancing or declining; but no one on earth can tell you, with any certainty, when that moment will be.

As previously stated, one should avoid investing in individual stocks because it is nearly impossible to do so consistently or profitably. Of course, early investors in companies like IBM or Apple made great fortunes, but buying the one lottery ticket with the winning numbers might also result in substantial wealth. The risk in selecting the one exceptional stock is great, as are the odds stacked against you of hitting the jackpot.

As with individual stocks, the Law of Inertia applies to mutual funds; but funds provide greater safety. If a few stocks in a fund don't perform as anticipated it will rarely sink the entire fund. There is definitely safety in numbers.

Experience indicates that momentum investing in funds—specifically sector funds—will result in the greatest opportunity for success. Sector funds are those that comprise stocks representing a single, specialized area of investment, and as such, they are riskier than an index fund that may invest in an entire market. However, funds that concentrate on one area of the market tend to do much better (or sometimes much worse) than the market as a whole. That is simply the nature of specialty funds.

Most financial companies offer sector funds, but the company with the greatest variety is Fidelity Investments, whose more than fifty individual specialty funds cover every sector from Banking and Electronics to Multimedia and Pharmaceuticals, and from Canada to Japan. There is always one sector or another doing well, and even when the entire market collapses there are always the Select Gold and Select Utility sectors that may actually thrive.

Fidelity, and most other financial companies, makes it fairly easy to determine which funds are doing best. Go to Fidelity.com and follow these directions:

Click on **Research** in the green box at top.
Scroll down to **Mutual Funds** and click.
Click on **See Results** at lower right green button.
Click on **Fidelity Funds Only** at left column.
Click on **YTD (Daily)** column.

All funds appear rated by year-to-date performance.
Those who begin their investment at the beginning of the year, when current results may be undependable, should refer to the **1 yr** column to identify funds that have appreciated the most during the previous year. Select the first few funds provided they are not all concentrated in one related group, such as, for example, Health Care, Medical Delivery, and Medical Equipment. If several are in roughly the same area you might eliminate one or more of these choices. There is rarely a need to select more than five to ten funds for your portfolio. Those with the best, current year-to-date record are the ones you want to hold.

Unlike the S&P 500 or the Dogs of the Dow strategies, which require little attention, the Momentum strategy obliges you to check periodically to see how they're doing. As a minimum you should check every couple of weeks and record the current year-to-date progress of your funds. In that way you will discover which are moving up and which are going nowhere. If you continue to monitor the Fidelity website you will also know when funds you don't own suddenly surge ahead of those you do own. When it appears that one of your funds lags a better one that you do not own, that is the moment to switch out of the laggard and into the one performing better.

At what point should you switch funds? That is a matter of judgment, of course, but if there is a fund that outperforms the year-to-date performance of your worst fund by about ten percentage points or more, consider switching out of your worst fund and into the outperforming fund.

You should be aware that most Fidelity Select funds assess a penalty if you trade a fund in fewer than thirty days. Realistically, it may take that long to determine how the fund is performing. The point is to give your funds a chance; some may be slow to move, which doesn't necessarily mean they should be dumped. Don't let your eagerness—or anxiety—lead to overtrading.

Because of the mechanical nature of the Momentum strategy the last thing you should worry about is in which areas of investment you should be. Some investors have a bias against industries like tobacco, alcohol, gambling, and defense, popularly known as *"butts, booze, bets, and bombs"*. Avoidance of such companies may depress these stocks in the short run, but make them attractive in the long run. Funds that concentrate on "sin" stocks have outperformed the S&P 500 Index by nearly two percentage points during the past decade. And they have done even better against the so-called "socially responsible" funds.

Some say that investing in what is generally unpopular may be one of the most rewarding strategies. In fact, the more people hate an industry the cheaper the stocks in that industry become—cheap enough to offer lasting value. So put your biases aside. No need to check your moral values at the door, but you will do better if you pursue funds that are advancing, regardless of their holdings.

If, for example, the Defense fund is moving up that's all you need to know. You're now in Defense. Ignore the dreadful implications of war. Defense companies may profit from wars, but they don't start them. Wars result from the political decisions of others. What should concern you is the direction of the fund; if it is going up, so, very likely, is your net worth.

8

VARIATIONS ON A THEME

I'd like to live as a poor man,

with lots of money.

Pablo Picasso

There is another momentum investment strategy worth considering, and that strategy involves the entire world of mutual funds, as well as a specific holding period similar to the Dogs of the Dow. Janet Brown, a San Francisco fund manager, suggested some years ago that investing in the funds of just one financial company needlessly eliminated most existing mutual funds. Her preference was to identify the best performing funds, regardless of which financial company managed them, what stocks they owned, and even their annual expenses, since that was already reflected in their returns. Her results over the past twenty years topped the Standard & Poor's 500 stock index by between three to five percent, making this a strategy that you might seriously consider.

Every variation of momentum investing, including this one, relies on a phenomenon known as "persistence of performance", which is another way of expressing Sir Isaac Newton's Law of Inertia. In other words, stock funds that perform well over a period of time generally continue to be superior performers in the near term. Rather than selecting from fifty Fidelity Funds, however, one may now choose from thousands of funds held by dozens of companies.

One identifies and purchases equal dollar shares of the top five, no-load, mutual funds that are outperforming all others. You hold these funds for a maximum of one year and then replace them with funds that are performing better. There may be one or two funds that carry over for another year, if they continue to outperform, but as in the Dogs of the Dow, you periodically replace the laggards with the new outperformers.

Now, you may ask, how does one find the best performing funds? There are several web sites that list the historic movements of mutual funds, such as Barchart.com, Morningstar, Yahoo, and Fidelity Investments. This strategy requires more time than the others, because one must identify the five funds with the best year-to-date or twelve-month trailing performance. These five funds may be general, specialized, global, or whatever; you are only interested in how they performed. It doesn't matter what stocks they hold, who manage them, or even their annual expenses, so long as they are no-load funds.

It should be noted that the Wall Street Journal lists the best monthly performance of funds just after the first of each month. The *Category Kings*, as they are called, include Large Caps, Midcap Value, Sector Funds, etc., etc. This is a valuable resource for quick comparisons among funds and may benefit an unsuspecting investor with a suddenly brilliant idea.

Your selected funds will be held for a set period of time, as you would the Dow Dogs. The length of time may be three months, six months, or at the most a year, at which time you review the world of funds again and replace your laggards with better performing funds. Some believe that you should hold the funds until another fund you do not own appreciates at least ten percent more than your worst performing fund, regardless of the length of time you've held the one you are selling. There is a good chance this time period would be at least a month or more.

You should be aware that dealing with five or more separate fund companies will generate a blizzard of paperwork, as well as consume more time than with the other strategies previously discussed. Those who find satisfaction in creating this kind of investment portfolio will be happy to spend whatever time it takes. Others, however, may not find it nearly as pleasant as reading a book, watching a ball game on TV, or taking a nap. That is understandable, and for those so inclined, we advise sticking with the S&P 500 or the Dogs of the Dow strategies. They will get rich more slowly perhaps, but they will avoid uncertainty, anxiety, and most other discomforts along the way.

9

MONEY MAKES THE WORLD GO 'ROUND

Money is like sex–

only too much is enough.

John Updike

The intent of this concise book is to improve your investment results, whether or not you understand how markets actually work. Its larger purpose, however, is for you to increase your net worth more easily in order to enhance your life. Yes, more money generally improves one's life, and that is why everybody–rich, poor, and in-between– wants more of it.

So, one might ask, how much money is enough? John Updike suggests, "only too much is enough". Many apparently agree. In Forbes latest annual listing of the country's 400 wealthiest people an individual had to be worth one-and-a-half billion dollars to be on the list. (That's *Billion* with a *B*.) Imagine that! The lowest person on the totem pole of affluence was worth a mere $1,500,000,000.

Have you any idea how much a *billion* is? It looks like a one followed by nine zeros, but what does it represent? A billion minutes ago Jesus was alive. A billion months ago dinosaurs roamed the earth. If a billion one-dollar bills were placed end-to-end, they would stretch around the equator nearly four times, and would weigh a thousand tons! And that's just *one* billion. Bill Gates has 79 billion, Warren Buffet, 72 billion, and each of the Koch brothers, 43 billion.

One can hardly imagine that magnitude of wealth, and most would agree that no one needs an amount that cannot be spent in several lifetimes. As the boxer, Floyd Mayweather expressed it, "Once you get to a certain point you can't spend it all; there's nothing more left to buy."

Nevertheless, in the tradition of our commercialized culture every citizen is encouraged to become as rich as possible. Money has become more important than ever and perhaps *the* most important element in today's society.

At the same time, social responsibility continues to struggle in an uphill battle. Consider this: In the past fifty years the compensation ratio of Chief Executive Officers to workers in this country has gone from 20 to 1 to nearly 300 to 1. In some cases workers can't afford consumer products being manufactured by their own companies.

So, you may ask, who cares? We all know life can be unfair and that some people are treated more equally than others. That's not exactly news. Well, here's something to think about: The ebb and flow of world events, government policies, corporate practices, and the basic values of our society directly affect *all* our lives, and that includes the way we earn, manage, and spend our money.

Though income inequality has become a serious concern there are certain workers who have actually thrived in the new profit-oriented society, and they are principally in the entertainment industry. Clearly, consumers will spend any amount of money to be entertained. Fifty years ago television was free. Of course there were only five or six channels, and you needed an antenna on your roof to access them. But free meant that it cost you nothing.

Cable companies today have scores of channels catering to every special interest, but the monthly tab can run to hundreds of dollars. And have you noticed the number of commercials on television these days? Twenty-five percent of all TV is now advertising. Why? Because money makes the world of television go 'round.

Cable access has led to an explosive interest in sports, which has resulted in more professional sports coverage than ever before. With greater sports exposure has come another explosion, this time in athletes' salaries. Who would believe that a boxer could earn two million dollars for one fight or a tennis player three million for one tournament?

Virtually all sports are sustained by advertising money, which has resulted in nearly forty end-of-the-year bowl games, such as, for example, the Allstate Sugar Bowl, played in the Mercedes-Benz Super Dome in New Orleans. There's little question that money makes the entire world of sports go 'round.

A more serious concern is the matter of who rules our country. A recent edition of *Perspectives on Politics* claims that ordinary Americans have virtually no influence on our country's national policy. It is wealthy individuals and business-dominated interest groups that shape policy outcomes. The interest of ordinary citizens was considered by the studies to be "non-significant".

An old saying, *"Money talks"*, means that when you slip the maître d' a fifty dollar bill you will generally get the best table in a crowded four-star restaurant. Subtle and not so subtle bribes have always tempted authority figures like city councilmen, building inspectors, highway patrol officers, and others who accept payoffs for preferential treatment. But the Pandora's box the Supreme Court opened with the Citizen's United decision–inadvertently or otherwise–engineered a system of bribery that resulted in a virtual corporate takeover of American political views.

New ways are constantly being devised for Lobbyists and Political Action Committees (PACS) to accept millions for political candidates. The amounts are huge, often anonymous, and unsupervised. This is an activity with which individuals simply cannot compete. Even more dubious is the practice of Congressional members who join lobbying groups after completing their term of office. Those who follow that career path earn an average pay raise of 1000 percent or more. It goes without saying; money–above all else–makes the political world go 'round.

Income inequality has produced an American society of haves and have-nots. The wealth disparity has never been greater, as the top one percent of earners now control nearly half the wealth of our country. Most of the 99 percent, however, are not exactly destitute; they're just not in the top one percent. Some at the bottom may be homeless or hungry, but most are what we call average, middle class Americans.

To be in the one-percent club takes a yearly income these days of about half a million dollars. That's a lot of money, but to characterize all people who earn that much as privileged elitists would be a mistake. You cannot assume that all prosperous people are arrogant and uncaring. They are, in fact, the very people who finance museums, concert halls, university buildings, art galleries, and scholarships. Wealthy people are nearly the same as everyone else; except of course, they have more money.

On the other hand, we must recognize the growing disparity between rich and poor. And we must also recognize the seriousness of a persistent middle-class decline. A large, vibrant middle class has always been fundamental to maintaining a free society. Every major company listed on every Stock Exchange began in a middle-class basement, garage, or modest middle-class storefront. A strong middle class assures that society will advance and that anyone can accumulate capital. And that leads to a more vigorous market where all investors have an equal opportunity to prosper.

Stock markets function as a microcosm of life itself. Investors listen to opinions of analysts and experts, but it is the investors' reactions to that information that count. The ultimate value of an investment is determined by the beliefs, biases, and emotions of the millions engaged in trading.

Investors' personalities range from daring, thrill-seeking cowboys to those quietly sitting in their rockers on the front porch knitting scarves. Both may own

> *An investment, like life, is unpredictable.*

shares in the same company, but how will they react if poor corporate earnings are announced? Will they sell, buy more shares, or take a nap? That's what determines the daily value of an investment. Like life itself—it is unpredictable.

So what has any of this to do with making more money in the stock market? Simply this: A person can beat the market without understanding the first thing about it, but that same person is obliged to pay attention to significant developments that affect his or her financial life, as well as the financial lives of those around us.

Money does indeed make the world go 'round, that much is clear; but one should realize there is more to life than money. In an ideal world we should strive to be responsible citizens and show compassion to one another. That is something money can't buy.

In the meantime, save, invest, succeed, and make your life—as well as the lives around you—more pleasant.

10

FINAL THOUGHTS

If you think nobody cares if you're alive,

try missing a couple of car payments.

Earl Wilson

Though people regularly discuss the markets and economic matters, it remains an odd fact of life that people resist speaking about money itself. Money is considered a dangerous subject to be carefully avoided in polite conversation—more so than even politics or religion. Most feel that revealing facts about personal finances is as uncomfortable as undressing in front of total strangers. Likewise, the people who ask how much you earn or the cost of anything you own are considered boorish, if not outright rude. There is nothing more personal than one's money.

Most parents keep financial details hidden from their children for most of their lives. Even when children reach an age of awareness and ask, "Are we rich?" many wealthy parents avoid further discussion by answering, "Not really; we're simply comfortable."

> *Nothing is more personal than one's money.*

It's a bit different with politicians, of course, because most people don't trust politicians. So it has become common for presidential candidates to submit several years of personal income tax returns, which probably prove little more than they paid taxes. If the money on which they were taxed, however, came from operating an illegal cock-fighting operation you'd never know it.

In concluding this brief book I'd like offer some further words of advice. I've been an active investor for most of my adult life. In addition, I've participated in real estate ventures, managed an educational company for architectural license candidates, (which, unexpectedly, turned out to be my paper-bag machine) and, for the most part, pursued the professional career for which I was trained. In all these activities I've made a number of faux pas, as you now know. Happily, however, I've done more things right than wrong, and as a result, I've enjoyed the benefits of financial success.

So, you may wonder, what have I learned about the markets after all these years and what investment secrets might I share with you?

Unfortunately, I have no secrets. In fact there *are* no secrets. Anyone might accomplish what I did by following the simple strategies in this book and having the patience to allow market forces to work their happy magic.

All the information required for successful investing is available to everyone and easily accessed on a computer. The only inside information possibly offering you an advantage over others resides in corporate boardrooms. If, for example, you have a relative sitting on the Board of Directors of a publicly traded company ply him or her with several spiced martinis at your next Thanksgiving dinner. You might very well come away with information that could be profitable. It might, however, land your relative in jail if the story becomes widely known.

The personal experiences that follow, both of which happen to be true, illustrate the vagaries of insider trading.

Several years ago an architect friend was designing a new home for the Corporate President of a publicly traded Electronics Company. During one of their many conferences the architect asked the client if he thought it would be wise for him to invest part of his architectural fee in stock of the client's company. The client believed that would be a great idea, because they were about to report extraordinarily good earnings. The architect revealed the story to me, we both purchased shares of the company, and both of us made a substantial profit on our investment.

Another story involves an old high school friend who had become head of the Legal Department of a publicly traded conglomerate dealing in financial and insurance products. We sometimes met for lunch, during which he regularly reported on the immense success his company was enjoying. When I asked if he thought I should buy shares in the company, he was encouraging and thought it would be a splendid idea.

A day or two later, while still considering my decision, the company collapsed–virtually overnight–in a massive scandal. It seems their computer system had been cranking out thousands of fictitious insurance policies for years. My friend knew nothing about the deception, and in fact, ultimately lost a personal fortune in company stock he owned. Twenty other employees were convicted of fraud, and most ended up in jail. As for me, I dodged a fatal bullet.

As to investing in general–there is only one reason to do so, and that is to make a profit. Moreover, it is to make a greater profit than you could make by personal effort alone. In other words, your investments may quietly appreciate–with little involvement on your part–while you pursue a totally unrelated full-time career.

Regarding the subject of risk–all of life involves risk. For example, the simple act of getting out of bed in the morning is considered a low risk activity, but there have been instances where some leap out of bed, land awkwardly, and end up with a broken ankle. So one person's low risk may turn out to be another's crippling accident.

There are many levels of risk, and not all are bad. If you walk across a busy street against a red light you are taking a foolish risk; but if you bet two dollars on your favorite jockey you can only lose two dollars, not your life. Because everyone's risk tolerance differs, you might seriously think about your tolerance to risk before making an investment, just as you would before bungee jumping off a bridge.

If you are looking to make a quick killing, it can sometimes happen, but you must take extraordinary risks that often lead to financial suicide. The investment methods proposed in previous chapters of this book involve relatively minor risks, although they do require patience.

And while on the subject of patience, you should realize it is one of the most valuable of all investor qualities. Those, with unfortunate timing, who trade too soon or too late, may often lose huge amounts of money. But so what? There may be times when it is more profitable to simply do nothing. There is no penalty for taking a walk around the block when everyone is yelling at you to "DO SOMETHING NOW!" Remain calm and carry on, as they say. The markets will be there tomorrow, next week, and even next year.

A few more miscellaneous thoughts:

- It is an absolute fact that no one on earth can predict with unequivocal certainty what the markets will do on any given day. The closest anyone has come was J.P. Morgan, who said, "The markets will fluctuate." Those claiming to know better are either seeking attention or perhaps are high on drug-laced brownies. You should avoid dealing with people like that.
- Human nature rarely varies; thus markets are consistently driven by fear and greed.
- Just because an investment is doing poorly doesn't necessarily mean it can't do worse.
- Never fall in love with an investment. It makes your spouse jealous and often leads to financial loss.
- Don't let commissions or other fees concern you; they are part of the cost of doing business. There are more important things to worry about.

- As for professional advice: Most investment advisors are right, but only for about the last 20 percent of an investment's move.
- Tips are rewards for good service. Avoid the other kind from all sources; most are not worth knowing.
- Your investments should never keep you awake at night. You should sell your holdings down to the sleeping point no later than the following morning.
- Lastly, if it sounds too good to be true, it very likely is.

There is little more I can I tell you. You probably know as much now as I, and with patience and fortitude your investment results should match or even exceed mine. That is my hope and expectation.

"Now, let us all be happy and live within our means,
even if we have to borrow money to do it with."

Artemus Ward

www.ingramcontent.com/pod-product-compliance
Lightning Source LLC
Chambersburg PA
CBHW030901180526
45163CB00004B/1651